Microwave Cookery

Your Questions Answered

Microwave Cookery

Your Questions Answered

Jan Harris

ANGELL EDITIONS
Newton Abbot, Devon

First Published October 1985
Reprinted March 1986
Reprinted August 1986
Reprinted April 1987
Reprinted December 1987
Reprinted May 1988
Reprinted December 1988

Line illustrations by Evelyn Bartlett

Printed in England
by Vine & Gorfin, Exmouth
for Angell Editions Limited
39 Coombeshead Road, Newton Abbot, Devon

British Library Cataloguing in Publication Data
Harris, Jan
    Microwave cookery: your questions answered.
    1. Microwave cookery
    I. Title
    641.5'882   TX832

ISBN 0 948432 00 4

Contents

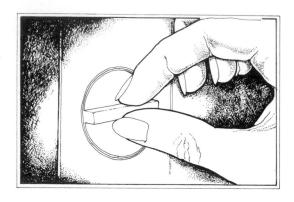

Are Microwaves Safe?

Microwave ovens have been the subject of much discussion regarding safety. When reading this section it will become very apparent that in many ways a microwave oven is the safest of all methods of cooking. Experts state that the chances of health damage from a microwave oven today are akin to receiving a suntan from the moon!

1   *Q.* Are microwave ovens built to a higher degree of safety nowadays?

   A. Yes, most machines have six different safety factors. If in doubt always look for British Electrical Approval Board (BEAB) approval or the British Standards Institution's 'kite-mark'.

2   *Q.* What would happen to the food if there was a power failure?

   A. Exactly the same as to conventional cooking, the food would be partially cooked. When power became restored cooking could be completed, but with a higher degree of satisfaction as microwaves sterilize food instantly, leaving no nagging doubts about bacteria.

3   *Q.* Is it possible to put one's hand in the microwave whilst it is working?

   A. No. Microwaves are automatically switched off when the 'door-open' operation is touched.

4   *Q.* Will the door leak in time?

   A. No. During manufacture the door is opened and closed on test machines 30,000 times.

5   *Q.* When I leave the machine at night should it be switched off at the plug?

   A. No. In many machines this would mean setting the clock daily, and is unnecessary unless the microwave is being left for long periods such as holidays.

6   *Q.* What happens to the microwaves? Are they still in the food after cooking?

   A. Microwaves are little pulses of energy which are used up on the heating process and disappear completely. To prove this, place a light-bulb in $\frac{1}{2}$ cup of milk and switch your microwave oven on HIGH for $1\frac{1}{2}$ min. The bulb will light up. Switch off the machine and the bulb will go out, proving no microwaves are left in the milk. IMPORTANT: prolonged, repeated use of this test will damage the machine.

7   *Q*. Where does the heat come from?

A. Microwaves, when passed through food, make activity in the moisture molecules of the food. The intense activity creates friction—friction cooks the food.

8   *Q*. Why don't the microwaves pass through the door?

A. Microwaves travel in straight lines bouncing off the cavity walls but not moving in a forward direction. There is a very fine metal mesh in the door to deflect the rays in an improbable isolated situation.

9   *Q*. What is the expected life of a microwave oven?

A. A microwave oven should last for many years. As with other appliances, all parts are replaceable over a reasonable period.

10   *Q*. What is likely to go wrong?

A. The magnetron is the most important part of a microwave oven, and is generally guaranteed for up to three years.

11   *Q*. Could I repair it myself?

A. No, it would not be wise.

12   *Q*. Could I buy parts to do so if I wished?

A. Yes.

13   *Q*. Does a microwave oven need regular servicing

A. Yes, every two years.

14   *Q*. What would a service consist of?

A. Checking all main parts, testing the magnetron etc.

15   *Q*. Does the timer automatically switch off at the end of each cook-cycle?

A. Yes, on all machines available.

16   *Q*. My husband has a heart-pacemaker fitted. I am told microwaves can affect the workings of it; is this true?

    A. Heart-pacemakers have been known to be affected by microwaves, but also there are many such users who are not affected. It is best to check with your medical specialist prior to purchase.

17   *Q*. Is it dangerous to put metal inside the microwave oven?

    A. No, not at all, but it would damage the machine considerably.

18   *Q*. If I accidentally left a spoon in a dish during cooking, would it spoil the machine?

    A. All of us at some time or another leave metal in the microwave. Isolated incidents will not do much harm but metal in prolonged contact with the microwaves will in time damage the oven.

19   *Q*. Should food be removed from the microwave oven as soon as the machine switches off?

    A. It doesn't matter one way or the other. Microwaves continue to cook for a few moments only and food will then cool naturally whether in the microwave oven, or out of it.

20   *Q*. Does microwave leakage cause cancer?

    A. No. Obviously microwaves are a form of radiation and in quantity would be very harmful; but the very, very miniscule amount of leakage from a microwave oven is insufficient to be harmful, and indeed is less than emitted from a colour TV.

21   *Q*. Does the microwave oven automatically switch off?

    A. Yes, immediately the door-release operation is touched.

22 *Q*. What happens to the microwaves when the door is opened?

A. They are already 'used up' such is the speed of microwave activity.

23 *Q*. Why don't plastic dishes melt?

A. Because microwaves pass straight through any substance but metal therefore there is no direct heat on the dishes, only the heat transferred from food being cooked.

24 *Q*. What harm would be caused if someone inadvertently started the microwave oven by mistake?

A. If, for a prolonged period, microwaves are bounced into the cavity without moisture to work on, or 'use' them up, the microwave oven's magnetron could be damaged. Always leave a cup of water inside the oven when not in use.

25 *Q*. Is it safe to allow school-age children to use a microwave oven?

A. Yes, probably far safer than allowing them to use a conventional oven or hob.

26 *Q*. I noticed steam escaping from the outside of the oven door. Is the microwave safe to use?

A. Yes, perfectly. Steam escapes by travelling around edges of the door. Microwaves travel in straight lines only, and are therefore barred.

27 *Q*. Will oven gloves protect my hands from microwaves?

A. There is no need to protect your hands, as there is no contact with microwaves. When the microwave oven door is opened the microwaves have already disappeared.

28 *Q*. If I fit my microwave on a shelf under a food cupboard in which I keep breakfast cereals, would the steam from the oven affect them?

A. No, there is not sufficient steam escaping from the door to do this.

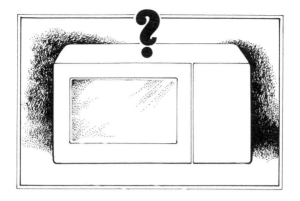

Buying a
Microwave Oven

If you are thinking of buying a microwave oven, some basic prior knowledge is essential, and will save considerable time. The information gained from reading this section will enable you to shop with confidence.

29 Q. Why do the prices of microwave ovens vary so?

A. Because the machines are all so different; go to a specialist for help when selecting a machine. Firstly the power output which governs the speed of microwave cooking varies tremendously. The 500 watt is the lowest and is rapidly becoming outdated. Cookbooks for it are not readily available and, because its speed of cooking is now slow in comparison to that of its speedy rivals, probably no new books will be written and most of the books now available are outdated. The 500-watt machine generally is very small with no stirrer fan, sometimes no turntable and often no heat settings, therefore it is cheaper. The 600-watt machine commands a slightly higher price, but still often lacks some of the necessary facilities. I would recommend 650-watt machines as the simplest to operate, and there are many books written for this power. This is a choice of facilities. Some machines have touch controls; can be programmed to switch on automatically when you are out; cook by weight—you feed the machine the information as to weight, type of meat etc. There is even a machine which 'knows' what vegetables you are putting in and how many! As a general rule, the more sophisticated automation, the more you pay.

30 Q. I cook for two people only. What output power should I buy?

A. 600 to 650 watts.

31 Q. I cook for six, which oven would you recommend?

A. 650 to 700 watts. Higher power means quicker cooking per 450g (1lb).

32 Q. How much does a microwave oven, cost to run per hour?

A. Just 4p.

33 Q. Is it cheaper to boil a kettle than to use a microwave oven?

A. No, microwave is cheaper, particularly when only one cup of water is necessary. How often do you fill the kettle and only use part of the water?

34 Q. Is a microwave cheaper or more expensive to run than a gas or conventional electric oven?

A. Much cheaper, costing only 4p per hour. In addition, food is cooked quicker and therefore much less fuel is used.

35 Q. I live alone. Would a microwave oven be justified in cooking for one person only?

A. In terms of time-saving and fuel economy, microwave cooking holds benefits for all. There is no warm-up time for the oven, no huge cavity to heat to temperature before cooking commences. Family-sized meals can be prepared, divided into four portions, and frozen until required.

36 Q. Where is the best place to position a microwave oven?

A. On a worktop, eg fridge or freezer; built into a cupboard; anywhere in fact that is convenient to you. But do not place a microwave too near to conventional cooking appliances, if such appliances remain in use. Heat could damage the microwave casing.

37 Q. How much space is necessary around the cabinet?

A. Sufficient for air to circulate, about 25mm (1in–1¼in) all round.

38 Q. How simple a matter is it to 'build in' a microwave oven to a unit?

A. Provided the electrical supply is available, very simple. If the kitchen fitter cannot supply a fix-in surround, most microwave-oven manufacturers sell them.

39 *Q.* Is it all right to use adaptors in an electric wall-point to which a microwave oven is connected?

A. No. Allow one plug per socket for the microwave power point.

40 *Q.* Is a turntable really necessary?

A. Yes, it certainly saves a lot of time opening and closing the door to turn the food. Also it avoids the need to be in the vicinity of the kitchen whilst the microwave is cooking.

41 *Q.* Is a turntable better than an antenna underneath?

A. Yes. The cook pattern is far greater. A machine that has a stirrer fan in the roof of the oven in addition to the turntable gives the very best possible results.

42 *Q.* Is the top of my medium-height fridge a safe place to stand the microwave oven?

A. Yes. Microwave ovens are made with non-slip rubber 'feet' which are set in from the edge of the microwave for stability.

43 *Q.* Some machines have a probe; what is it useful for?

A. Cooking stews, casseroles, jams, joints of meat, milk puddings etc. The probe is pushed into food (it may be sellotaped in place), and the machine is set to a 'temperature' setting rather than the usual microwave 'time' setting. When food reaches the correct temperature, the probe switches off the microwave oven.

44 *Q.* What is variable power?

A. Variable power is the name given to the function of different heat settings. Simply, it operates thus. If HIGH is selected, the machine is switched on fully for the time given. If ROAST is selected, the machine switches on for 50 sec and switches off for the remaining 10 sec in every minute of the time selected, thereby food does not get quite so hot as when using full power. For DEFROST the machine is on for 30 sec, off for 30 sec in every minute, and so on.

45 *Q.* Are machines with automatic settings superior to manual machines?

A. Some are, some aren't. Make quite sure before purchase just what all those settings are for, and whether your household requires them all. Generally a manual machine is better for someone who is around the house for a good proportion of the day. Also cookbooks are more readily available for manual machines.

46 *Q.* What are the advantages of a touchbutton microwave oven over a manual machine?

A. Generally speaking—programmability; to be able to order the machine to control itself without having to be in the kitchen to do so.

47 *Q.* Is a stainless-steel interior better than acrylic?

A. Yes, stainless steel is easier to clean and will last much longer.

48 *Q.* I have read that quite the most important feature of a microwave oven is the door. Which type is best?

A. A metal-edged door, rather than plastic, set into a deep recess.

49 *Q.* Are some microwave ovens noisier than others?

A. Yes. Try to see the machines working before purchase, to enable the best choice to be made.

50 *Q.* What is the importance of cubic capacity of the microwave oven?

A. Unlike a conventional cooker where the whole oven is heated, a microwave oven creates heat only inside food. You cannot use the whole of the cavity, although some manufacturers claim you can! Microwaves cook on a power output/weight ratio, and if you crammed the oven cavity to capacity 11.3kg (25lb) of food could be contained. At approximately 8 min to 450g (1lb) (assuming all the food was suitable for cooking on HIGH), it would take 3 hr 20 min to cook it all! Therefore there is no advantage to have a huge capacity oven over a smaller one as it will still take the same amount of time as if foods are cooked separately.

51   *Q.* Some microwave ovens have 'browners'. If this is necessary, why don't all microwave ovens available have the same facility?

A. Most machines with 'browners' are combination ovens giving facilities for both microwave and conventional cooking. This type of machine is generally sold to persons intending to dispose of conventional cookers. Foods which require browning after microwave cooking can be placed under the grill for completion.

52   *Q.* Is it difficult to clean a combination oven?

A. Yes. More so than a microwave oven as fat splashes burn on.

53   *Q.* What power supply would I require for a combination oven?

A. 13amp supply.

54   *Q.* Why do some microwave ovens have shelves?

A. Generally, the machine with shelves is very high-powered and suitable for warming-up food and defrosting only. Such machines are usually found on commercial premises.

55   *Q.* I would like to reorganise my kitchen and dispose of my cooker, which microwave oven would you recommend?

A. There are models available that have the facilities of both the microwave and the electric fan-assisted oven. Look for one that *combines* the two together as the time saving is tremendous. One such machine will happily cook a 1.4kg (3lb) joint of meat with potatoes (beautifully crisped and roasted) for four, in 45 min from a cold start! It may be used as an independent microwave cooker, as a convection hot-air fan-assisted oven, or successfully combines both together.

56 *Q.* If I buy a microwave oven to replace my existing cooker, will I need a hob?

A. No, with organization you could well manage without; but most people prefer to have conventional cooking as well.

57 *Q.* What other electrical equipment would be useful as a back-up?

A. A toaster, a deep-fat fryer and a mini-boiler for eggs (the type used in hotel bedrooms for quick cups of coffee).

58 *Q.* Does it matter where my machine is situated in the kitchen; can it be put in the larder for instance?

A. Wherever you find is most convenient will be suitable for the microwave oven, provided sufficient air is allowed to circulate around the outer casing—25–30mm (1–1¼in) all around is acceptable.

59 *Q.* Is there a machine produced that has a right-hand door opening?

A. Not to my knowledge.

60 *Q.* I would like to buy a combination oven. What troubles me is how long it would take to repair if it went wrong, and how would I manage without it?

A. Microwave specialist repairers give precedence to such users and would normally fix it within 24 hours.

61 *Q.* How heavy is a microwave oven?

A. About 13.6–22.7kg (30–50lb). One side, generally the right-hand facing, is much heavier than the other.

62 *Q.* How does a microwave save time on washing up?

A. There are *no* saucepans. Food is often prepared and eaten in the same dish and there are no burned-on stains.

63 *Q.* Compared to conventional cooking is the food as high in nutrients after cooking in the microwave oven?

A. Higher. Food is cooked so quickly that there is less loss of nutrients.

64 *Q.* How would I know when the microwave oven has finished cooking?

A. A bell or buzzer informs you.

65 *Q.* How is food kept hot whilst the next part of the meal is cooking?

A. It is unnecessary to keep food hot, as the microwave oven can be used as an instant warmer-upper prior to serving the completed dish.

66 *Q.* How would I get all the food in at once in odd-shaped dishes?

A. You wouldn't. The easiest method would be to fill a large flattish dish with vegetables, chops on top etc, then reheat all together, and serve them from the dish. Alternatively, plate up individual meals and reheat.

67 *Q.* I have a commercial premises serving large quantities and large dishes of food. Is there a higher-powered machine available?

A. Yes. Commercial ovens start at 700-watt output and go up in power to 2kw, which reheats a pizza in 10 sec!

68 Q. How long a guarantee is generally given with a microwave oven?

A. Usually 2–3 years on the magnetron, 1 year on parts and labour.

69 Q. Is there an optional extended warranty of 1 year for parts and labour, with 2 or 3 years' cover on the magnetron?

A. An additional option on service cover for up to 5 years is usually available at varying prices. Generally the microwave specialist engineer's premium is slightly higher, but better value as most cover *all* parts inclusive of glass turntable, tray and light-bulb.

70 Q. I am deaf and cannot hear the bell 'ping' at the end of a cooking cycle. Would I still be able to use a microwave oven?

A. Yes. The light inside the machine switches on whilst food is cooking and off when the machine has finished.

71 Q. I am considering replacing my basic microwave oven, which is 500-watt power. Since higher-power ovens are more expensive, would they be more 'efficient'?

A. No, the actual power governs the speed at which food can be cooked. Generally speaking the newer machines are more efficient because of turntables, variable power and programmability.

72 Q. What could I easily cook in an oven with variable power that I cannot cook in my machine with COOK/DEFROST?

A. Stews, casseroles, milk puddings, all cheaper cuts of meat, joints of lamb, ham etc.

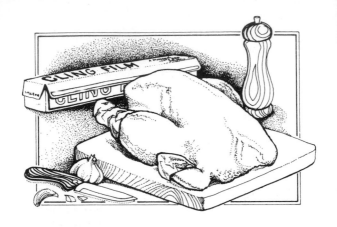

Tips for the New Microwave Cook

With everything, there is a right and wrong way to work, and microwave cooking is no exception. The questions and answers in this section will prove an invaluable short-cut to successful results for beginners.

NOTE: All timings are approximate, as there are so many variables in microwave cooking. Power outputs, for instance, differ considerably from one manufacturer to another. The actual temperature of the ingredients will also affect cooking times; for example, cakes made from margarine from the refrigerator will take longer to cook than if the margarine used was at room temperature The density of food is also very important; chunky pieces of meat will take longer to cook and defrost than wider flatter pieces of equivalent weight. Another variable factor is the age and freshness of fruit and vegetables; older vegetables have tougher skins.

Timings throughout the book are for a 650-watt power output machine. For 700-watt power deduct $\frac{1}{7}$ of the time stated; for 500 watts add $\frac{1}{4}$. Defrosting times are altered in a similar manner.

·73 *Q.* How should I clean my microwave oven?

A. Damp cloth and kitchen paper only.

74 *Q.* Should I pierce a hole in cling-film?

A. Yes, unless your oven is a sensor-type machine, when you should not.

75 *Q.* My machine has an auto-sensor and the instructions state quite clearly that I should cover all dishes with cling-film and not pierce a hole. Why

A. The sensor works by measuring humidity and moisture present in the food during cooking, and it is necessary to 'seal' the dish for the sensor to work accurately. Cling-film is a very good medium for this, but it is generally agreed that a three-piece dome-dish set (see Question 124) does the job more efficiently.

76 *Q.* If I cook food in a pudding basin, will it take longer than in a casserole dish?

A. Yes, as there is no lid to a pudding basin, and also because its greater depth to area causes food to be piled up.

77 *Q.* Why do some foods of the same weight take longer to cook?

A. If food is thick or chunky it will take longer than if in thinner, flatter portions, since microwaves have easier access to the food and not so much density to work through.

78 *Q.* Why is it necessary to have a cup of water in the microwave oven whilst drying herbs or melting chocolate?

A. Because there is insufficient moisture for the microwaves to be absorbed into, and this could result in the microwave oven being damaged.

79 *Q.* Could I start off food in the microwave oven prior to barbecueing, to speed things up?

A. Yes, a good idea; three-quarter cook everything! This will also prevent burning the outside of food on the barbecue, whilst still achieving the charcoal flavour.

80 *Q*. Can I sterilize the baby's bottle?

A. Yes. Wash thoroughly, rinse out and shake dry, microwave on HIGH until warm and dry.

81 *Q*. Can I use aluminium foil in the microwave oven?

A. Yes, but with caution, and in the opposite way to conventional usage. Microwaves cannot penetrate metal and therefore foil is used to *prevent* microwaves from cooking food, such as wing tips on a chicken, which may overcook if not protected. *Never* allow foil to touch any part of the microwave oven.

82 *Q*. What would happen if I did use metal dishes?

A. The microwaves would bounce off the dish, and would therefore be unable to cook food properly. Also the machine could be damaged.

83 *Q*. I have an old microwave cookbook which mentions equalizing time. What is it?

A. Standing time.

84 *Q*. What is standing time?

A. Standing time is over-emphasised in certain cookbooks, and is only relevant to certain foods, eg meat and cakes. The heat generated inside the food is so intense that even after the machine is switched off, food still cooks from within. Experience soon tells when standing is beneficial.

85 *Q*. When I leave food to stand for the allotted time, should I leave it in the microwave oven?

A. It doesn't matter either way, but of course it is useful to be able to use the oven for other dishes during the standing time.

86 *Q*. In my microwave cookbook it states 'P.L. 4' and 'P.L. 3', what does this mean?

A. Power Level 4 and Power Level 3.

87 *Q.* Can I make tea in the microwave oven?

A. Yes. Boil water in a ceramic pot and make tea as normal.

88 *Q.* If microwaves pass through lids of dishes, why is it necessary to cover food?

A. Heat builds up inside and food cooks quicker, also the oven stays clean and the food retains moisture.

89 *Q.* When I need to use the timer on my manually operated microwave oven, the timer doesn't seem to work on 30 sec; why?

A. On manual timers it is necessary to turn the timer past 3 min then back to 30 sec.

90 *Q.* My microwave has variable power, can I set the dial between marked settings ie SIMMER/ROAST?

A. Not always, but generally it is possible with machines marked with variable power settings HIGH, MEDIUM, ROAST, SIMMER, DEFROST etc.

91 *Q.* I am told that wine bottles may be sterilized in the microwave oven. How?

A. Simply cleanse and rinse bottles, shake as dry as possible, remove excess moisture from outsides, and lay on their sides in the oven, using HIGH setting heat until bottles are warm and dry—a few minutes only.

92 *Q.* How should I convert family recipes for one portion?

A. There is no hard and fast rule, as recipe conversions for the microwave vary from dish to dish. Far better to cook the whole amount and divide into four dishes for freezing or reheating.

93 *Q.* My family is very fond of fish and the microwave oven cooks it superbly. My only complaint is the smell left inside after cooking. How can I freshen up the machine?

A. Cut a juicy lemon in half. Using both halves, rub round the oven cavity. Leave juice for a few seconds before drying thoroughly with a paper towel. If smell persists, repeat the process.

94 *Q.* If I enrol in classes for microwave cooking, would the timings be correct for my oven?

A. Specific information for each class member's oven should be given.

95 *Q.* Can you recommend a good cookbook?

A. Not without knowing the power of your microwave oven. Power is most important when choosing cookery books.

96 *Q.* Where can I get help with the cooking queries that are raised daily?

A. Microwave specialists throughout the country run cookery lessons, as do manufacturers. Some local radio stations have regular phone-in programmes.

97 *Q.* Can I cook packet soups in a microwave oven?

A. Yes, but make up and leave to stand 15 min before cooking. *Mix very thoroughly* and cook on HIGH for 4–5 min, stirring twice.

98 *Q.* How would I cook prepared boil-in-the-bag meals?

A. Snip the corner of the bag and put the bag into a dish to catch spills. Cook on HIGH without first defrosting. Trial and error is needed for timing; try half the conventional time to start with.

99 *Q.* Can I make filter coffee in the microwave oven?

A. Yes, there are special coffee makers for the microwave oven. Alternatively make it conventionally and reheat by the cup for 2 min approximately.

100   *Q*. Can I make sauces in the microwave oven?

     A. Yes. Make in the same way as conventionally (see *Q*. 335 where instructions for Cheese Sauce are given).

101   *Q*. If I find that food is not cooked enough, can I put it back into the oven and give it more time?

     A. Yes.

102   *Q*. How can I stop milk boiling over?

     A. Always use a jug or container of twice the capacity of the liquid measurement.

103   *Q*. Can I use ordinary recipes in my new microwave oven?

     A. Yes, eventually, but it does take time to achieve the ability to do so. Trial and error is the usual route.

104   *Q*. Can I mull wine?

     A. Yes, give it 2 min on HIGH per 550ml (1pt).

105   *Q*. If I cook a casserole, the dish becomes very hot; yet if I use the same dish for warming up cooked food, it remains cool. Why?

     A. Dishes are heated by food, not by microwaves; therefore if food is intensely hot over a relatively long period, dishes will become hot too.

106   *Q*. Why do some foods need covering, not others?

     A. Microwaves pass through all lids of dishes and affect only the food, yet heat rising from the food is trapped by the lid and combines to cook food faster. Most dense or chunky pieces of foods need covering, thinner food will cook uncovered.

107   *Q*. Is it safe to use metal spoons when stirring food?

     A. Yes, but do not leave the cutlery in the oven during cooking.

108   *Q*. Would it be better if I used wooden spoons or plastic?

A. Yes, neither of these would adversely affect the oven if left inside during cooking, though possibly the plastic spoon would melt slightly and distort.

109 *Q*. Why should I use cling-film, but not foil?

A. Cling-film is plastic, with no metal content, therefore invisible to microwaves. Foil is metallic and microwaves cannot penetrate it.

110 *Q*. Some foods, a stew for instance, take so long that I find it quicker to use a pressure cooker.

A. A pressure cooker will cook stews quicker than the microwave; however, the microwave preserves nutrients and flavour, and at only a fraction of the cost of using a pressure cooker.

111 *Q*. What foods require covering during cooking?

A. Meat, fish, poultry and vegetables; also pasta, rice, and suet mixes.

112 *Q*. What cannot be cooked in a microwave oven?

A. Yorkshire puddings, pies, boiled eggs, roast potatoes, any deep-fat fried foods.

113 *Q*. Will the microwave oven toast bread?

A. No.

114 *Q*. Is it possible to fry food using the microwave oven?

A. Yes, using the browning dish, which is a frying-pan substitute.

115 *Q*. My fairly old microwave oven does not have variable power. How can I overcome this?

A. With difficulty, but it's not impossible. Cook food in 5 min intervals, alternating between HIGH and DEFROST, HIGH and DEFROST. This is suitable for joints of meat, cheaper cuts of meat and fruit cakes.

116 *Q*. How do I defrost frozen butter?

A. Heat for 20 sec on HIGH setting.

117 *Q.* Can I use the DEFROST setting to cook on?

A. Yes, it is useful for stews or slow cooking.

118 *Q.* Why shouldn't I add salt to food before cooking?

A. You may, diluted in water, or stirred into food; but never sprinkle directly onto food as this will encourage the food to dry out and spoil the appearance and taste.

119 *Q.* I make a very tasty quick curry on my conventional stove top, using cooked chicken. Could I make the same dish in the microwave?

A. Yes. Cook onions first, then add remaining ingredients. Cook on HIGH for about half the conventional cooking time.

120 *Q.* How much food can be cooked at any one time?

A. As much as the machine will hold but, remember, the larger the quantity the longer the cooking time.

121 *Q.* Can I make jam in the microwave oven?

A. Yes. As a general guidance prepare fruits and sugar as in conventional recipe. Always use a 2.3 litre (4pt) vessel to make 1.4kg (3lb) maximum. Soften fruit first, before adding sugar and water. Use HIGH setting. Times vary from 20 to 30 min, depending on fruit.

122 *Q.* If I really overcooked food and dried it up completely, would it damage the oven?

A. In an *extreme case*, yes, but only if food is totally dehydrated.

123 *Q.* How easy is it to convert conventional recipes for microwave use?

A. There is no golden rule regarding conversions and each recipe must be approached differently. Whilst it is not difficult to convert recipes, a lot of experience is needed.

Dishes

It has never been so important, in any other form of cooking, to have the right equipment for the job. Whilst most people will know that metal dishes are not suitable, few beginners are sure of which dishes are, or how to improvise.

Always use the correct dish as advised.

124   *Q*. Which is the most useful dish to purchase?

     A. Undoubtedly a three-piece dome-dish set complete with a rack and tray which, when turned upside down, provides a 2.3 litre (4pt) covered casserole dish.

125   *Q*. What dishes can't I use in the microwave oven?

     A. No metal dishes at all. Ironstone, lead crystal and gold-rimmed crockery cannot be used either because of the metal content. Melamine— due to porous nature of the material.

126   *Q*. Is it all right to use bone china in the microwave oven?

     A. Yes. Any dish without a metallic edging or content, is fine. Remember though, exceedingly hot food may crack delicate dishes.

127   *Q*. Why can't I use the dishes I usually use?

     A. Microwaves cannot penetrate metal and therefore will cook food unevenly. To test dish suitability, put some water in the dish. If the dish gets hot before the water, it is not suitable for microwave cooking.

128   *Q*. Are Pyrex dishes suitable?

     A. Yes, Pyrex dishes are ideal for use in the microwave.

129   *Q*. Is it suitable to use ironstone pottery?

     A. No. Any dish with a metallic substance is definitively unsuitable.

130   *Q*. Is melamine a type of plastic, and should I use it?

     A. *Melamine* is a type of plastic, but *no do not use*. It is porous and will therefore become very hot during use and will spoil.

131 *Q.* I read somewhere that I can cook in glass, surely this would break if heat was applied?

A. Microwaves ignore every substance except metal and moisture, thereby passing through every other material as light passes through a window. However, if water was poured into a glass then heated in the microwave to boiling point the glass would shatter; but due to the boiling water, not the microwaves. The temperature of the food is the dominating factor.

132 *Q.* I bought some special plastic microwave containers for cooking vegetables. There are no lids supplied and cling-film doesn't stick to them.

A. Put a dinner plate on top when food needs to be covered during cooking.

133 *Q.* I have a collection of large paté dishes from the supermarket. Are such dishes suitable for use in the microwave oven?

A. Paté dishes are excellent.

134 *Q.* What if my dishes haven't got lids?

A. Use a dinner plate. This serves two purposes: it warms a serving plate in addition to solving the lid problem.

135 *Q.* Are square or round dishes more suitable for use in the microwave oven?

A. Circular dishes are better.

136 *Q.* I have read that cakes should not be cooked in square dishes. Why?

A. Microwaves pass more evenly through a circular dish. Corners create areas of concentration from two sources and cakes tend to dry out in those places.

137 Q. I have noticed that if I make a dish, other than sponge pudding, in a basin it takes longer. Why?

A. Because food is heaped up in a pudding bowl and therefore the microwaves take longer to work through the food. Flatter, shallower dishes are best.

138 Q. Are there special 'roasting' and 'boiling' bags purely for use in the microwave oven?

A. No. Use ordinary cooking bags.

139 Q. How should I use roasting bags?

A. Roasting bags are most effective when used to roast a joint of meat or poultry. The bag creates a self-basting effect, and helps to aid browning.

140 Q. All the roasting bags that I have purchased have metal ties supplied. I cannot use them, what should I use?

A. Elastic bands or clear adhesive tape.

141 Q. When I used a roasting bag, it ballooned up. Would it alter the cooking time if I punctured it?

A. No, a small hole in the top is necessary.

142 Q. Do I need lots of special new dishes?

A. Only two—a browning dish and a meat rack. Improvisations can be made using ice-cream tubs and similar containers, though freezer-to-microwave ovenware is inexpensive and readily available.

143 Q. Is a browning dish essential?

A. If you like fried foods, yes.

144 Q. How do I clean a browning dish?

A. Clean, whilst still hot, with cream cleanser and nylon pot brush.

145 *Q.* I have a very small microwave oven and have only seen large browning dishes. Are there small sizes available?

A. Yes. Corningware make a No 9 size which fits very small machines.

146 *Q.* When I used my browning dish a huge dark stain appeared. Is it damaged?

A. No. It is not damaged but you have allowed the dish to become very dirty by not cleaning properly after use.

147 *Q.* When I used the browning dish exactly according to the manufacturer's instructions, the food didn't brown. Is the dish faulty?

A. No, probably the instructions are Heat the dish with oil added. After preheat time the oil is hot in addition to the dish, and results then are good.

148 *Q.* What would happen to the browning dish if it was overheated?

A. It would break.

149 *Q.* Is there danger if the browning dish is overheated?

A. Yes, fat could ignite. Also the glass turntable could shatter.

150 *Q.* What is the advantage of using the lid on the browning dish?

A. It stops fat splashing and cooks food quicker, but will detract from the browning and crisping if used whilst frying foods.

151 *Q.* Should I use HIGH power whilst using the browning dish?

A. Heat the dish using HIGH power. Food can be cooked on MEDIUM/ROAST once dish has been heated.

152   *Q*. If I buy a browning dish will I be able to cook a chicken in it?

A. No, only chicken joints, steaks, chops etc; nothing larger.

153   *Q*. Can I use a Pyrosil dish instead of the browning dish? It looks the same.

A. No. The browning dish is a special type of dish, with a metallic coated base-plate which reflects microwaves and heats up rapidly, unlike the Pyrosil dish which would remain cold.

154   *Q*. Can I use paper plates?

A. Yes, throwaway plates are very useful.

155   *Q*. Do I require a meat thermometer?

A. My personal advice is 'no'. Find out the power of your machine. If it is 650 watts, place meat on a rack, rub salt into fat only, cover and cook on HIGH for 1 min for 450g (1lb) then 12 min per 450g (1lb) on MEDIUM or ROAST setting. Reduce this time for other than well-cooked meat.

156   *Q*. Do dishes get hot from the food?

A. Yes, due to heat transference a dish will get quite hot if the food being cooked is in contact with it for any length of time.

157   *Q*. I have a combination oven using microwaves and conventional fan-assisted heat. Can I use metal dishes in this machine?

A. When using the oven on *convection* only. Some manufacturers state that their machine can take metal dishes on *combination* but, as microwaves cannot penetrate metal, cooking cannot be as efficient as when using Pyrex or earthenware.

158   Q. Can I use plastic dishes in my combination oven?

A. Certain plastic microwave dishes available can safely be used in combination or convectional parts of the combination cooker to temperatures of 205°C (400°F).

159   Q. I tried to make fairy cakes but they fell flat in the papers. How can I make them keep shape?

A. There are purpose-made dishes called muffin pans, or bun trays. Alternatively cut plastic drinking cups down to half size, using one cup and individual cake paper-lining per cake.

160   Q. Are there any family-sized dishes available to fit on a turntable?

A. There is a dome-dish which takes 2.3 litres (4pt), and is complete with lid and roasting rack.

161   Q. My microwave oven is a combination of convection and microwave. What dishes can I use?

A. Pyrex, pottery or earthenware are ideal for use with both

162   Q. Are there different types of roasting racks?

A. Yes, but they all do the same job and only one is necessary.

163   Q. My combination oven has a wire rack. Can I use it for bacon?

A. Yes.

164   Q. Can I use the rack from the combination cooker in the microwave part also?

A. Yes.

165   *Q*. Can I use metal dishes in the combination part of my microwave oven, whilst using microwaves?

A. Yes, but better results would be obtained by using pottery or Pyrex.

166   *Q*. Why do I need a roasting rack?

A. Microwaves work on moisture. If a joint of meat was cooked on a plate, part of the joint would be immersed in juices; meat needs to be raised up to ensure even cooking.

167   *Q*. Can I use the rack for anything other than joints?

A. Yes, for beefburgers, fish fingers, tomatoes etc.

168   *Q*. Can I use the roasting rack for cooking cakes?

A. Yes.

169   *Q*. Where can I buy accessories?

A. From department stores, microwave oven specialists and by mail order.

Defrosting

The DEFROST facility of a microwave oven realises the true potential of the freezer. The combined use of these appliances will revolutionize mealtimes.

170   *Q.* What is the secret of successful defrosting?

     A. Work by weight; at 650 watts give 8 min per 450g (1lb).

171   *Q.* Can all foods be defrosted in the microwave oven?

     A. Yes. Microwaves defrost quite naturally.

172   *Q.* Do all microwave ovens defrost?

     A. Yes. Some of the older machines do not have a DEFROST setting, but if the oven is switched on and off at 30 sec intervals, defrosting will be satisfactory.

173   *Q.* Do all foods need to be completely defrosted prior to cooking, or can some foods be cooked from a frozen state?

     A. All frozen vegetables may be cooked without prior defrosting, also beefburgers, small whole fish, fish fingers, fish cakes, fillets of fish, kippers etc.

174   *Q.* If I prepare a plated meal for the freezer, can I leave it frozen as long as if it were cooked traditionally.

     A. Yes. To serve, reheat on HIGH setting without prior defrosting.

175   *Q.* What would happen to the food if I defrosted on HIGH by mistake?

     A. It would start to cook very unevenly around the outside, and food would be cooked at the edge but frozen solid in the centre.

176   *Q.* Why does a square block of frozen food take so much longer to defrost than similar weight and type of food frozen in a larger flatter dish?

     A. Microwaves have easier access to flatter dishes and do not have to work through food that is piled up or presented in a smaller deeper receptacle.

177   *Q*. Is it completely safe to defrost seafood using the microwave oven?

A. Yes, totally safe. Many restaurateurs deliberately use the microwave oven to ensure that food is sterilized.

178   *Q*. How should I defrost a trout?

A. Cooked from raw or frozen on HIGH setting, a 225g (8oz) trout will take 4 min. If wished, cook on HIGH for 1 min to start defrosting, then stuff the trout or add garnish. Continue cooking for 3 min or until cooked through.

179   *Q*. Is it necessary to defrost frozen vegetables before cooking?

A. No. Follow microwave cooking instructions for fresh food, but allow half as much time additionally.

180   *Q*. My microwave-oven cookbook supplied with the machine suggests defrosting a chicken on a roasting rack placed on the turntable direct. Surely the water will overflow?

A. No, surprisingly enough there is very little water left after defrosting. Most of it evaporates during the process.

181   *Q*. Whenever I defrost a chicken in the microwave oven, the inside cavity remains icy. If I persist and add more time, the outside starts to cook. How do I avoid this?

A. Defrost according to the manual supplied with the machine. At the end of this time rinse the carcase with cold water and allow to stand on a rack for 8–10 min.

182   *Q*. Can I defrost fresh cream cakes?

A. Yes, but exercise caution, using DEFROST setting 30 sec–45 sec at a time.

183 *Q.* How should I defrost frozen pastry?

A. With care. Use the DEFROST setting and check that pastry is not allowed to get even slightly warm.

184 *Q.* If I accidentally turned the cook button on instead of DEFROST, and the chicken I was defrosting started to cook, would it be safe to eat when completely cooked?

A. Yes, provided the poultry was completely cooked in the microwave oven, as food is sterilised during cooking.

Reheating

Food that has been reheated in a microwave oven loses nothing in the way of colour, texture or flavour. Also the nutritional value of food that has been cooked and reheated in the microwave is still higher than for meals cooked and served straightaway in the conventional manner. Therefore reheating can be done with complete confidence as an integral part of the microwave way of cooking.

185 Q. Is it safe to reheat *all* leftovers?

A. Yes, food is sterilized instantly.

186 Q. Should food be covered during reheating time?

A. No, this is unnecessary. Microwaves penetrate the covering and cause a 'steamed' effect if the covering is tight.

187 Q. When I reheat cooked food in my microwave oven, parts of the meal are hotter than others. Why?

A. It is due to the distribution of the microwaves inside the oven. Most probably your machine has either a fan or a turntable, not a combination of both. Turning the plate once would help considerably.

188 Q. What would happen to a plated meal if it were reheated more than once?

A. There would be little or no change and it would be edible. In practice this should not be necessary as a meal takes only a matter of minutes to heat precisely when required.

189 Q. How long will a plated meal take to reheat from the freezer?

A. Nothing varies so much as individual portions of family meals for, like everything else concerned with microwave cooking, weight is the dominant factor. Allow 5–9 min from frozen, 4–6 min if just taken chilled from refrigerator. Remember, better too hot than too cold. Food won't spoil if you add more time.

190 Q. Can I reheat mince pies from the freezer?

A. Yes. Using HIGH setting, and allow 30–45 sec each from frozen. A plate of 6 pies will take 2½–3 min.

191 *Q.* When reheating soup I find it is always cold in the centre. Why?

A. The centre is always the last part of the food to heat up. Stir once during cooking.

192 *Q.* Is it really quite safe to reheat pork in the microwave oven?

A. Yes, everything that is cooked or reheated in the microwave is sterilised instantly due to the intense heat that is generated inside the food.

193 *Q.* How long would it take to reheat a 2.3 litre (4pt) family-sized frozen casserole.

A. Allow 14–18 min on HIGH setting, *do not defrost first.*
Foods that have been cooked, then frozen, can quite safely be reheated on a HIGH setting. The DEFROST setting is important to use on frozen uncooked foods because of its pulsating action of switching on and off, thus ensuring that frozen foods do not start to cook on the outside whilst still frozen in the centre.

194 *Q.* When I reheated baked beans, they popped open and made a mess. Why?

A. Because you overheated them! The contents of a small tin takes only ½ min on HIGH setting.

195 *Q.* If I prepare a 'ready meal' and leave it in the fridge, the gravy appears to soak in. Should I reheat it separately?

A. Yes, for absolute perfection. I use yoghurt pots for this purpose, and never waste any gravy at all. Gravy can be frozen and reheated.

196 *Q.* How long will it take to reheat a bought Christmas pudding?

A. Allow 3–4 min for a 450g (1lb) size, 5–6 min for a 900g (2lb) size.

197 *Q*. Which is the best way to heat a pizza?

     A. On kitchen paper, placed on a roasting rack.

198 *Q*. When I reheat ready cooked pastry it collapses and becomes soggy. Is there a remedy?

     A. Pastry should be reheated for the absolute minimum of time. Always make a hole or two in the top of a pie to allow hot air to escape whilst heating; a knife blade does this effectively without spoiling the appearance. It will also assist if the pie is placed on an open roasting rack, allowing air to circulate underneath.

199 *Q*. Could I leave a whole egg-and-bacon breakfast to reheat?

     A. Yes, but fried egg should be left on a saucer separately. Heat breakfast for 1–2 min, heat egg only for 15–25 sec *maximum*. Serve egg on top.

200 *Q*. Is it possible to reheat fish and chips, and should I remove the wrapper?

     A. Fish and chips may be reheated exactly as purchased, ie in paper.

201 *Q*. How can I stop a skin forming on custard or sauce I wish to reheat later?

     A. Place a circlet of dampened greaseproof paper on top of jug.

202 *Q*. Can I take the chill off my cat's food taken from the fridge?

     A. Yes; 15 sec per portion maximum.

203 *Q*. Can I put two plates in the oven at once to reheat?

     A. Yes, there are purpose-made plastic ring-stackers available. Up to three meals may be heated at once.

Meat and Poultry

Contrary to general belief, meat and poultry can be cooked with complete success using the microwave oven. A roasting rack is absolutely essential.

204   *Q.* My recipe book suggests cooking a chicken inside a roasting bag, yet the manufacturer's instructions suggest using a rack; which is best?

    A. Both together! Place chicken in roasting bag, puncture holes in the bottom of the bag, stand bird and bag on a roasting rack for cooking.

205   *Q.* What is the spice that browns a chicken?

    A. Paprika is excellent, or there are purpose-made food colourings available.

206   *Q.* If I use conventional stuffings for my poultry, will it take longer to cook?

    A. Yes.

207   *Q.* Is it in order to put stuffing into poultry before roasting?

    A. Yes. Calculate the cooking time per 450g (1lb) after stuffing the bird.

208   *Q.* How can I make the chicken look appetising?

    A. Brush carcase of bird with oil or margarine, sprinkle liberally with paprika or chicken seasoning, cover and cook. Poultry cooked this way really does look brown and deliciously appetising.

209   *Q.* Is it possible to cook pheasant in the microwave oven?

    A. Yes, unless there is a lot of buckshot visible there should be no problem. Cook as for chicken—8 min per 450g (1lb) at 650-watt power.

210   *Q.* When I cooked a turkey the meat around the leg shrunk away.

    A. The thinnest part gets the greatest concentration of microwaves, try covering such parts with aluminium foil *Do not allow foil to touch sides of oven.*

211 *Q.* What is the largest size of turkey that can be cooked in a microwave oven?

A. Obviously this depends on the size of the oven. Usually a 650-watt machine will take up to a 5.4kg (12b) bird. Check to see if your machine has a fan or prism in the roof of the oven, allowing turntable to be dispensed with or turned upside down to enable a larger dish to be used.

212 *Q.* How would I cook a joint of meat using the microwave oven?

A. Wash meat, pat dry with kitchen paper, weigh, sprinkle salt onto *fat only*, brush all over with oil. Wrap in roasting bag, make holes in top and base, place on a roasting rack. If you have a dome set, use it. Cook meat on HIGH for 1 min per 450g (1lb). Then reduce setting to ROAST or MEDIUM for 11–12 min per 450g (1lb). Reduce these times for rare cooked meat, as these timings are for well-done joints.

213 *Q.* How would I seal a joint of meat prior to roasting?

A. Heat the browning dish with 2–3×15ml tbsp (2–3 tbsp) oil on HIGH for 7 min. Roll joint in sizzling fat and microwave for 30 sec intervals until edge of meat has changed colour.

214 *Q.* My microwave oven has a ROAST setting, so why doesn't it brown?

A. 'Roast' is the term for cooking meat, slightly slower than FULL power. Rub salt into *fat only* and cook meat on a rack to improve the colour.

215 *Q.* How can I achieve pork crackling?

A. Remove 'rind' from pork and rub salt into both sides. Secure rind to joint with wooden cocktail sticks. Cook joint on a rack following cookbook instructions, then remove the crackling and cook it on a rack separately for a further 5 min.

216 *Q.* If microwaves cook from the inside out, how can I cook rare beef?

A. Microwaves do *not* cook from the inside out, but start at the outer edge of the food and work inwards. Food, however, is cooked from within its own skin, which causes confusion. Cooking rare beef, therefore, is simple—just reduce cooking time per 450g (1lb).

217 *Q.* Is it possible to cook Yorkshire pudding in the microwave oven?

A. No. Cooking Yorkshire pudding is one of the microwave oven's few limitations.

218 *Q.* I always cook roast potatoes with a roast joint. If the roast potatoes have to be cooked conventionally, what is the point of cooking the meat in the microwave oven, when it could all be cooked together?

A. Food is more nutritious cooked in the microwave oven. Also, if preferred, meat and potatoes may be part-cooked in the microwave oven prior to conventional roasting, thus reducing shrinkage and expensive conventional cooking time.

219 *Q.* How should I cook best steak?

A. Steaks cook with or without a browning dish. Allow 6–7 min per 450g (1lb) for well-done steaks; 4–5 min per 450g (1lb) for rare to medium; 1 min per 450g (1lb) for rare.

220 *Q.* I am experiencing difficulty when cooking chops; they are always tough and dry.

A. Dryness means overcooking. Aim to cook until blood traces are *almost* gone. Remove from the microwave oven and, by the time you have served the remainder of the meal, the chops will have completed cooking from the heat within.

221 *Q.* Should I put oil in the browning dish before cooking chops?

A. Yes. Use 1–2×15ml tbsp (1–2 tbsp) and heat dish for 6–7 min.

222 *Q.* When I cooked liver it 'popped' and made a mess in the oven. Why?

A. Liver is covered with a membrane which, if not pierced before cooking, will expand and split. Simply prod liver with a fork prior to cooking.

223 *Q.* When I cooked minced beef according to instructions supplied, it went into lumpy pieces. Is this normal?

A. Yes, but can be overcome by breaking up with a fork during cooking.

224 *Q.* Why do some beefburgers cook quicker than others of the same weight, but of a different brand?

A. Beefburgers, fish cakes, fish fingers and sausages are to a large extent cereal. Different brands have varying amounts of cereals. The higher the content of meat or fish, the longer the cooking time.

225 *Q.* When I cooked rashers of bacon they were limp, pale and soggy, yet some I saw cooked at a demonstration were really brown and crispy. Why?

A. Most probably the demonstration bacon was cooked on a rack. If rashers are cooked directly on a plate, fat cannot drain away from the bacon so that it can crisp.

226 *Q.* In my cookery book supplied with the machine it suggests cooking bacon on kitchen paper. I find it sticks.

A. Kitchen paper is fine to use provided the rashers are removed immediately the bell 'rings', otherwise time is spent trying to separate the bacon from paper. Try using a rack.

227 *Q.* How would you advise cooking savoury bacon rolls using a microwave oven and do you have a recipe?

A. **Savoury Bacon Rolls**
225g (8oz) prepared sage and onion stuffing
8 rashers of streaky bacon, rind removed
8 wooden cocktail sticks

Divide stuffing into 8 portions. Wrap each portion in a rasher, secure with a cocktail stick. Place each savoury roll on a roasting rack. Cook on HIGH setting for 8–10 min (*makes 8*).

228 *Q.* Cooking sausages in the browning dish seems to take ages. Is there a quicker way?

A. Yes. Conventionally grill several kilos (pounds) of sausages together. Flat pack in family-sized portions, freeze until required, reheat from frozen on HIGH for 6–7 min per 450g (1lb), or alternatively grill until brown then microwave to cook through completely.

229 *Q.* How can I cook a steak and kidney pudding from raw in the microwave oven?

A. **Steak and Kidney Pudding**
450g (1lb) steak and kidney
275 ml (½pt) beef stock, or water and 1 beef stock cube
150g (6oz) self-raising flour
75g (3oz) suet
water for mixing
seasoning

Combine meat and stock together in a 1.1 litre (2pt) casserole dish. Cook on HIGH setting for 5 min. Reduce setting to SIMMER and cook for 1 hr 15 min.

Mix the flour and suet with the water to form a stiff dough. Leaving enough dough for a lid, roll out remaining dough on a floured surface to line 1.1 litre (2pt) greased basin. Fill the basin with meat and stock, sprinkle with seasoning and flour. Dampen the top edges of the pudding and cover with the dough lid. Cover with cling-film, slit the top to allow air to escape during cooking. Cook on HIGH setting for 6 min (*serves 4*).

230   *Q.* Is it possible to cook ham in a pastry case?

    A.   **Ham en Croûte**

       1.4kg (3lb) ham joint (soaked for minimum of
          8 hours in cold water)
       25g (1oz) margarine
       25g (1oz) lard
       150g (6oz) self-raising flour
       seasoning
       25g (1oz) crushed dried onion flakes
       4×15ml (4tbsp) water
       beaten egg
       paprika for colouring

Remove rind from ham and trim off all excess fat
leaving a thin layer only. Place ham on a roasting
rack. Pat dry with kitchen paper.

Crust

Rub fats into the flour and seasoning, add the
onion flakes, mix with the water to form a soft
dough. Roll out on a lightly floured surface, shape
into a circle large enough to cover top and sides of
the ham. Place pastry over ham, neaten the edges
and bottom. Brush the pastry with beaten egg,
sprinkle liberally with paprika. Cook on HIGH
setting for 5 min, then reduce power setting to
ROAST. Cook for further 30-35 min (*serves 8*).

231   *Q.* I would like to cook minced beef, but what
    happens to the excess fat?

    A. Cook minced beef, uncovered, for 3–4 min,
then pour off excess fat before continuing to cook,
covered.

           Savoury Minced Beef

       450g (1lb) minced beef
       1 onion, chopped
       350g (14oz) can tomatoes
       225g (8oz) mixed vegetables (frozen or fresh),
         diced
       150ml (¼pt) beef stock
       seasoning to taste

  Cook the mince and onion in a 1.1 litre (2pt)
casserole dish, uncovered, on HIGH setting for
5 min. Drain off surplus fat, add remaining
ingredients, mix well. Cook, covered, on HIGH for
5 min (*serves 4*).

232 *Q.* I find that stew takes a long time to cook. Why?

A. As with conventional cooking, stewing meat requires a long slow cooktime. About half the conventional cooking time is needed on average to get meat to tenderise. I make stews complete with dumplings at my leisure, then freeze them. Reheating takes approximately 15 min for a family-sized portion, from frozen.

233 *Q.* Why does it take so long to cook steak and kidney?

A. Whilst meat takes a very short time to actually cook (until no juices show), cheaper cuts of meat, as in conventional cooking require longer cooking to enable the meat to tenderise.

234 *Q.* How do I make a traditional stew with dumplings?

A. **Stew with Dumplings**
225g (8oz) stewing or braising steak
2 carrots
1 small turnip
1 parsnip
½ small swede
1 medium onion
1 leek
550ml (1pt) beef stock, or water and 2 beef stock
cubes
seasoning
flour to thicken

Dice meat and roughly chop all vegetables. Combine all ingredients except flour in a 2.3 litre (4pt) casserole dish with lid. Cook, covered, on HIGH setting for 8 min, then on SIMMER or LOW setting for 1 hr 15 min. Mix flour with a little of the gravy. Add to stew, stir well, then cook on HIGH for 3 min.

Dumplings
150g (6oz) plain flour
75g (3oz) suet
milk or water to mix

Mix all ingredients to form soft dough. Divide into 5 dumplings and add to stew. Cook on HIGH for 5 min (*serves 5*).

35　*Q*. How would I thicken a stew?

A. Gravy granules are marvellous; just sprinkle onto food and stir.

36　*Q*. Whenever I make gravy in the microwave, it forms lumps. Why?

A. The secret is in the mixing. Before adding the thickening agent to meat juices etc, make sure that there are no particles of powder unmixed or, for an infallible result, use gravy granules.

37　*Q*. If microwaves do not cook pies successfully, how can I overcome the problem?

A. Batch bake conventionally, freeze individually and, using the microwave, reheat from frozen as required.

Vegetables and Fruit

Fresh, well-cooked vegetables are a fine source of vitamins and goodness, and excellent value for money. Microwave-cooked vegetables have superb flavour, are speedily cooked to retain even more nutrients, and cooking methods are very simple.

38 *Q.* My family like 'crunchy' vegetables, cooked in the French manner. Is the microwave oven capable of cooking such foods?

A. Yes. It is a simple matter of reducing the time per 450g (1lb) of food.

39 *Q.* Can I add salt to my vegetables before cooking, since my recipe book advises adding salt after cooking is completed?

A. Salt sprinkled directly onto vegetables would cause the food to dehydrate and turn withered and brown. However, salt added to liquid and dissolved is a perfectly safe method.

40 *Q.* Is it necessary to add water to frozen vegetables?

A. No, unless large quantities are prepared together.

41 *Q.* Can I blanch vegetables?

A. Yes. Use 12mm (½in) water in bottom of dish, cover and blanch on HIGH for 4 min per 450g (1lb). Drain, cool and freeze immediately. Food can be blanched in boiling bags, frozen, and eventually cooked in same bags.

42 *Q.* Can I dry herbs?

A. Yes. Put herbs between two sheets of kitchen paper. Always put an eggcupful of water in the machine whilst drying herbs.

43 *Q.* Can I cook two vegetables together?

A. Yes, provided they are of the same type, eg parsnips and swede. Combined cooking of beans and carrots would not be possible. Generally there is no advantage in cooking vegetables together, as microwaves cook on a power-to-weight ratio and will take as long to cook together as if cooked separately.

244 *Q*. Then how do I keep the first vegetable hot?

A. There is no need to. Food can be reheated as required without detriment to flavour or appearance.

245 *Q*. Why do two potatoes take longer to cook than one?

A. Whilst cooking one item, all the microwaves produced are concentrated into this cooking. If two food items are cooked at the same time, the microwaves divide forces and therefore have twice as much heat to produce.

246 *Q*. How would I cook oven-chips in the microwave?

A. On kitchen paper using HIGH setting. Or, for really crispy chips, warm a browning dish for 6 min on HIGH, add chips and cook for 8 min per 450g (1lb).

247 *Q*. I boiled potatoes using the microwave oven, but it seemed to take longer than on the stove. Why?

A. You covered the potatoes with water, and this is unnecessary, 12–20mm (½–¾in) is all that is needed.

248 *Q*. I cannot master the art of cooking plain old-fashioned boiled potatoes; the results are dried up edges and hard middles. How is it done?

A. Use a wide flattish dish so that the potatoes are spread over it instead of piled up. Cook to manufacturer's instructions, or on HIGH setting for 12 min per 450g (1lb), 20 min per 900g (2lb) in 12–20mm (½–¾in) salted water. Before cooking commences, toss the water over the top of the potatoes making the tops wet. Always cover during cooking; if the dish has no lid, a dinner plate will do.

249 Q. Can I cook new potatoes in skins as boiled potatoes?

A. Yes. Cooking instructions are the same as for normal boiled potatoes with skins on.

250 Q. Whenever I cook cauliflower florets there are small black burn spots in places. Why is this and am I doing something wrong?

A. The small black burn spots appear on cauliflower when it is allowed to 'dry out'. This is easily rectified by sprinkling the water over the cauliflower prior to cooking. The moisture will protect the food from overheating in places.

251 Q. I cooked carrots in the microwave but the result was not good. The edges of the ones on top were rubbery, though the ones underneath were fine.

A. You did not sprinkle water over the tops of the vegetables prior to cooking.

252 Q. When I cooked minced beef with onions, the meat was completely cooked but the onions were crunchy. Did I do something wrong?

A. No. Onions take quite a long time to soften once added to other foods. Start them off first for a couple of minutes.

253 Q. How long does it take to cook corn-on-the-cob?

A. It takes 3 min if fresh; 4 min if frozen. Brush the cobs with butter. There is no need to cover frozen cobs, but fresh ones will benefit from sealing inside cling-film.

254 Q. Which is the best way to cook mushrooms?

A. Prepare and place mushrooms with stalks (broken off) in a dish with knob of butter, seasoning and 1×15ml tbsp (1tbsp) water. Cover and cook on HIGH for 3 min per 100g ($\frac{1}{4}$ lb).

255   *Q*. What is the best way to cook cabbage?

A. Shred cabbage and cook in a flattish container, covered, for 8–10 min per 450g (1lb). Halfway through cooking time, turn the bottom layers to the top of the dish.

256   *Q*. How can I make corn fritters?

A.   **Corn Fritters**
     4×15ml tbsp (4tbsp) oil for frying
     2×15ml tbsp (2tbsp) milk
     100g (4oz) self-raising flour
     seasoning to taste
     ½×5ml (½ level tsp) mustard powder
     2 eggs size 3, beaten
     100g (4oz) sweetcorn kernels

Heat browning dish with the oil added, on HIGH for 5–6 min.

Mix all other ingredients together to form a batter. When dish is heated, add a spoonful of the batter, cooking three in a batch for 2 min on HIGH setting turning over once. Serve brown side uppermost. A browning dish is essential (*serves 6*).

257   *Q*. Is it simple to make apple sauce using the microwave oven?

A. Yes. Core, and score around middle, 1 large cooking apple. Cook in a deep cereal bowl for 3–4 min on HIGH. When cooked, scoop out centre, sweeten and serve. For larger quantities peel, and slice as usual.

258   *Q*. How would I bake an apple in the microwave oven?

A. Core, and score skin around middle. Stuff centre with granulated sugar and cook for 3–4 min on HIGH.

259   *Q*. What would happen if I didn't score an apple around middle before baking?

A. Heat would build up from inside and the skin would split.

260   *Q.* Could I stuff the apple with sweet mincemeat before cooking?

    A. Yes. Alternatively, use chopped dates and walnuts, blackberries, etc.

261   *Q.* A 'quick tip' in my microwave cookbook suggests warming a lemon to make it more juicy. For how long?

    A. For 30–45 sec on HIGH, or until warm.

262   *Q.* Can I cook chestnuts in the microwave oven?

    A. Yes, score through skin around middle of each chestnut. Place on a glass tray and cook for 6–7 min per 450g (1lb).

Baking and Puddings

Making cakes and puddings is a simple process in the microwave oven. But be warned; there is no legitimate excuse for ever buying cakes and puddings again! This section is ideal for introducing the family to microwave cooking.

263   *Q.* When making cakes is it necessary to grease and flour dishes?

     A. Grease only.

264   *Q.* If I open the microwave oven door during the cooking of a cake, will it sink?

     A. No. There is sufficient heat within the food to hold its shape for several seconds.

265   *Q.* Should I turn cakes out immediately or leave them to stand in the dish?

     A. Cakes should be left in the dish for a few minutes, then turned out.

266   *Q.* How can I be sure that my cakes are cooked properly if the colour does not alter?

     A. A cake shrinks from the side of the dish when cooked. If a cake readily leaves the side when tested it is cooked, even if the centre top is slightly moist. The residue of heat from within the cake will quickly complete the cooking, without further microwaving.

267   *Q.* Why did the Madeira cake that I cooked rise unevenly?

     A. Because of the distribution of microwaves inside your machine. To assist more even cooking, try raising cake up on a rack or upturned cereal bowl.

268   *Q.* If I leave my cake to stand in accordance with the recipe instructions, there is a white gluey-looking film around the base when I turn it out of the container. Why?

     A. The film you mention is usually in evidence when using a plastic container. The heat builds up with steam and spoils the appearance of a cake. To rectify, leave to stand for 3–4 min only.

269   *Q.* When I use a muffin pan lined with paper cases for small cakes, each small base gets wet and the cake case becomes soggy. What can I do about it?

    A. Use two paper cases rather than one, and turn cakes out immediately.

270   *Q.* I have made many cakes using my microwave oven, but so far have not had much success when lining the dishes with cling-film as my cookbook advises.

    A. Use special microwave-type plastic dishes. Cakes will slip out with ease.

271   *Q.* I would like to make a simple cake in the microwave oven for my first attempt. What should I cook?

    A. Try a packet sponge. Use one of the larger packets rather than small square boxes, as the larger type is highly successful. Mix as instructions on packet using size 3 eggs, plus an extra 2×15ml tbsp (2tbsp) of liquid. Cook on HIGH setting, one half at a time, for 2 min each.

272   *Q.* I would like to make a Christmas cake in the microwave oven, but cannot find a suitable recipe for my 650-watt machine.

    A. The following recipe is excellent for use in any machine as it is cooked on DEFROST.

Christmas Cake

100g (4oz) butter
100g (4oz) dark soft brown sugar
2 eggs
$\frac{1}{2}$×15ml tbsp ($\frac{1}{2}$tbsp) black treacle
50g (2oz) glacé cherries, chopped
625g (1lb 6oz) mixed dried fruit
25g (1oz) nuts, chopped
grated rind of $\frac{1}{2}$ lemon and $\frac{1}{2}$ orange
150g (5oz) plain flour
12g ($\frac{1}{2}$oz) cocoa
$1\frac{1}{2}$×5ml tsp ($1\frac{1}{2}$tsp) mixed spice
2×15ml tbsp (2tbsp) milk or sherry

Cream butter and sugar until light and fluffy. Beat together the eggs and treacle, and gradually add to the creamed mixture. Wash the chopped cherries and toss in a little of the flour. Mix cherries, nuts, fruit, flour, cocoa and mixed spice together. Fold in, with the milk or sherry. Spoon into a 20–23cm (8–9in) round greased-lined dish and cook on DEFROST setting for about 38–40 min.

273 *Q.* I am experiencing difficulty in cooking a fruit cake; it is always soggy or sunk in the middle.

A. Always cook fruit cakes raised up on a rack to ensure even cooking. Soggy centre is due to faulty timing—a little more time is needed. If the problem recurs, don't despair; cut a circle of aluminium foil the size of the cake, with a centre hole the size of the 'sunken' part, and microwave until the centre is cooked. The outside will not then be overcooked.

274 *Q.* Can I brown almonds in the microwave oven?

A. Yes. Place on a rack between two sheets of kitchen paper. Put an eggcupful of water in the centre of the rack. Microwave on HIGH until almonds turn brown.

275 *Q.* Can I use my conventional cake recipes?

A. Yes, but always make mixture slightly more moist than for a conventional oven.

276 *Q.* Is a ring-type cake dish where the middle is missing best?

A. For an absolute beginner's first attempt, a dish without a middle is a foolproof way of making cakes. Obviously, if there is no centre to drop, it can't!

277 *Q.* I make delicious scones in the microwave oven, but the colour is disappointing. Is there any remedy?

A. Yes. Preheat browning dish dry for 5 min, then rub base over with buttered paper. Cook scones, turning once, for 3–4 min.

278 *Q.* Some books say that pancakes can be made in the microwave oven; other say they can't. Which is true?

A. Yes, pancakes can be cooked in the microwave oven, but a browning dish is necessary.

Pancakes
100g (4oz) plain flour
pinch of salt
1 egg size 3
275ml (½ pint) milk (or half milk half water)
oil for frying

Preheat browning dish on HIGH setting for 5 min. Sieve flour and salt together into a large mixing bowl, make a well in the centre of the flour, break in the egg and mix carefully with the milk to make a smooth batter.

Brush the base of the heated browning dish, pour in batter gently until spread to a tea-plate size. Cook on HIGH setting for ½–1 min, turn over; cook on HIGH setting for 20–30 sec. Repeat until all the mixture has been used (*makes 6*). Serve pancakes with lemon juice and sugar.

279 *Q.* Can I cook a pizza?

A. Yes. Scone based ones are most successful. Alternatively, a pan-fried suet base is delicious.

Katies's Pizza
Base
75g (3oz) margarine
225g (8oz) self-raising flour
1×15ml tbsp (1tbsp) herbs
milk for mixing

Topping
tomato purée, to taste
4 rashers bacon, chopped
1 medium onion, chopped
50g (2oz) grated cheese
knob of butter

Rub the margarine into the flour and herbs. Mix to a stiff dough with the milk. Preheat a browning dish for 6 min; lightly brush, whilst hot, with the margarine. Roll the dough on a lightly floured board to a circular shape to fit the browning dish, raise the edge of the dough with thumbs to form a ridge. Prick the base lightly, cook in the browning dish on HIGH setting for 5 min (*serves 4*).

Spread the cooked base with tomato purée. Combine rashers, onion and butter in a separate dish, cover and cook on HIGH for 4 min. Drain mixture with straining spoon, and place on top of tomato purée. Sprinkle the cheese over the top, return to the microwave oven for 2–3 min or until cheese has melted.

280   *Q.* Is it possible to cook pastry in the microwave oven?

    A. Yes. Pastry for quiches, flans or open tarts is successful. Mix with egg in preference to water.

281   *Q.* Is it possible to make a quiche in the microwave oven?

    A.   **Savoury Quiche**

Pastry
75g (3oz) margarine
175g (6oz) plain flour
water to mix
1 egg yolk

Filling
3 rashers bacon, chopped
½ onion, chopped
50g (2oz) mushrooms, sliced or chopped
25g (1oz) butter
2 eggs
150ml (¼pt) milk
seasoning
100g (4oz) cheese
paprika (optional)

Rub margarine into the flour. Mix with water to a dough and roll out on a lightly floured board to line a greased 20cm (8in) flan dish. Prick all over with fork. Brush base with egg yolk to seal. Cook on HIGH for 3–4 min.

Cook the bacon, onion and mushrooms with butter on HIGH for 4 min, covered. Beat the eggs and milk with seasoning. Add the bacon and onion mixture to the cooked flan case. Cover with the egg mixture. Sprinkle with the cheese. Cook for 10 min on HIGH setting. Sprinkle with paprika if liked (*serves 4*).

282 *Q.* Is it possible to get crispy pastry?

A. Reasonable results can be produced, especially for sweet-pastry open tarts. Make shortcrust pastry to normal recipe, but mix with an egg instead of water and add 1×15ml tbsp (1tbsp), heaped, of demerara sugar.

283 *Q.* Can I cook pastry puffs?

A. Yes. Roll out 225g (8oz) pastry, cut into strips 75mm×40mm (3in×1½in). Cook on kitchen paper, one at a time, for 45 sec to 1 min on HIGH setting. Allow to cool, then sandwich two together with a jam and fresh cream filling. Sprinkle icing sugar over tops for appearance.

284 *Q.* Can I make mince pies?

A.   **Mince Pies**
    75g (3oz) soft margarine
    150g (6oz) self-raising flour
    1×15ml tbsp (1tbsp) demerara sugar
    1 egg
    ⅓ jar mincemeat
    milk or water for brushing
    nutmeg
    demerara sugar for decoration

Rub the fat into the flour, add the sugar, mix well with the egg. Roll pastry out onto a floured surface. Cut into 18 medium-sized rounds plus 18 small biscuit-sized star shapes. Grease a muffin pan, line with 6 circle shapes. Cook uncovered on HIGH setting for 3 min. Fill each tartlet with sweet mincemeat. Cook on HIGH setting for further 1 min. Remove from the oven, turn tartlets out onto a rack to cool. Cook two further batches using the same method. Place a piece of kitchen roll paper onto a roasting rack. Place all 18 star shapes onto paper. Brush each with milk or water, sprinkle liberally with nutmeg for colour and demerara sugar for crispness. Cook on HIGH setting for 2 min or until tops are crisp. Place one star onto each tartlet to complete.

285 *Q.* I understand that microwaves do not crisp foods, therefore that flapjacks and biscuits must be cooked conventionally.

A. No, not true. Flapjacks are excellent. Refrigerator biscuits—the type mixed, rolled into a cylinder, left in the fridge overnight, then sliced like a cucumber before cooking—are very good too.

Flapjacks
3×15ml tbsp (3tbsp) golden syrup
100g (4oz) demerara sugar
100g (4oz) butter or margarine
225g (8oz) rolled oats
1×5ml tsp (1tsp) baking powder
½×5ml tsp (½tsp) salt
1 egg, beaten

Grease a 20cm (8in) round flat dish. Place syrup, sugar and butter or margarine in an ovenproof bowl, heat on HIGH setting for 2 min. Stir until sugar is dissolved. Add remaining ingredients and place in prepared dish, cook on HIGH for 4–5 min. Cut into fingers when cooled.

Crunchy Biscuits
150g (5oz) butter
225g (8oz) light soft brown sugar
1 egg, size 3
1×5ml tsp (1tsp) vanilla essence
225g (8oz) plain flour
1½×5ml tsp (1½tsp) baking powder
¼×5ml tsp (¼tsp) salt
50g (2oz) rolled oats
2×15ml tbsp (2tbsp) currants

Place butter in mixing bowl, soften for 45 sec to 1 min on HIGH setting. Add sugar, egg and vanilla, and beat until mixture is light and fluffy. Add all ingredients, mix well. Roll into 2×50mm (2in) wide cylinders, wrap in greased paper and refrigerate for 8 hr. Slice into 6mm (¼in) slices. Cook 6 biscuits at once directly on the greased turntable for 2–2½ min on HIGH setting.

286 *Q.* I have made several attempts to make a cake from the recipe book provided with my microwave oven and have tried using different shaped dishes; each time it is ruined. What am I doing wrong?

A. Circular cakes are the most satisfactory. The problem could be due to your machine, as each microwave oven varies slightly, even identical makes purchased on the same day. Trial and error is necessary to establish how much time to increase or decrease from the basic instructions.

287 *Q.* How can I cook dumplings?

A. Mix your favourite recipe and add to hot cooked stews, casseroles etc. Cook for 5 min on HIGH.

288 *Q.* Can I use my own Christmas Pudding recipe in the microwave oven?

A. Yes. Cook on HIGH for 5–6 min for 450g (1lb) size, 8–9 min for 900g (2lb) size.

289 *Q.* Is there any secret for making a crumble topping look appetising?

A. Yes. Use demerara sugar instead of caster.

290 *Q.* Is it possible to 'prove' bread?

A. Yes, in 30 sec bursts on HIGH until dough doubles in size.

291 *Q.* Can I warm bread rolls prior to serving?

A. Yes, for 30 sec on HIGH. Serve immediately.

292 *Q*. Is it possible to bake bread using the microwave oven?

A. Bread is quite successfully made, but will have the appearance of a bap, rather than a crusty or crispy texture.

293 *Q*. Can I make garlic bread?

A. Yes, as follows:

Garlic Bread
50g (2oz) butter
1 clove garlic, crushed
small sprig parsley, chopped
1 small French loaf

Blend butter, garlic and parsley together. Slice the loaf in half lengthways, spread with the garlic butter, wrap the whole loaf in kitchen paper. Heat on HIGH setting for 45 sec to 1 min.

Alternatively, slice the loaf into portions, still keeping the loaf joined at the base. Spread each slice with garlic butter. Heat in the same way.

294 *Q*. I saw a demonstrator make a Saucy Sponge from a packet. How long does it take?

A. Approximately 5–6 min on HIGH. Mix exactly as packet instructions. Use only one dish.

295 *Q*. How can I prevent the ends of a jam roly-poly becoming overcooked?

A. Make sure edges are as thickly rolled out as centre part. Wrap in cling-film over greaseproof paper to cook.

Jam Roly-poly
200g (8oz) self-raising flour
100g (4oz) shredded suet
jam for filling
1×15ml tbsp (1tbsp) caster sugar
½×5ml tsp (½tsp) cinnamon

Mix the flour and suet with sufficient water to form a soft dough. Roll dough out on a floured surface, shape into an oblong. Spread the dough with jam leaving a 12mm (½in) border all around the edge. Roll up like a Swiss roll, sealing the top and edges with milk or water. Place the roly-poly, top edge down, onto a sheet of greased greaseproof paper. Roll up loosely. Secure ends with rubber bands. Wrap the whole in cling-film. Cook for 8 min on HIGH setting. Unwrap and place on serving dish. Mix sugar with cinnamon and sprinkle over roly-poly (*serves 5*).

296 *Q.* Is it necessary to cover suet roly-polys?

A. Yes. Loosely wrap roly-poly in greaseproof paper; then wrap in cling-film, leaving room for mixture to rise.

297 *Q.* Why do the Victoria sponges that I have made turn out more like puddings than cakes?

A. Because there is no 'drying heat' applied to food. All heat comes from within the food, therefore food is often more moist. However, an excessively pudding-type texture is generally a sign of slight overcooking.

298 *Q.* Should I cook the two halves of a Victoria sponge together with one half on a rack, or one half at a time.

A. Cook the halves separately. This way both halves will be cooked correctly.

299 *Q.* How can I make a Victoria sponge look less pale and more attractive?

A. Add egg-yellow colouring to accentuate the natural colour, or food colourings such as pink or orange. Dust the top with icing sugar through a paper doily placed on top, or ice the cake.

300 *Q.* I made a sponge cake which turned out fine. After I left it to stand it had the texture of a trifle sponge. What went wrong?

A. Overcooking! Any cake that looks 'cooked' is overdone. Aim to have the top very mildly moist but not wet.

301 Q. I made a sponge cake. The recipe gave the time as 6 min on HIGH. The cake wasn't cooked in the time given, but I left it to stand for a while. The appearance did not alter so I cooked it for a further minute, but the outside was then too hard. What did I do wrong?

A. Next time, cook the cake for 6½ min on HIGH. By allowing the cake to cool during the standing time, it took some energy to heat the cake back to the temperature it would be at HIGH setting. The outside always cooks first, therefore the edges were overcooked.

302 Q. I have heard that steamed sponge puddings are absolutely superb when cooked in a microwave oven. Do I cover the top and stand the dish in water?

A. No, on both counts. Mix the pudding (100g (4oz) mix), ie 100g (4oz) flour, 100g (4oz) fat, 100g (4oz) sugar, 2 eggs, in a basin; stand it on a glass tray. Cook on HIGH for 5 min.

303 Q. When I cooked a sponge pudding it overflowed although I used the correct size of dish.

A. Microwaves have the ability to make puddings and cakes rise really high. Often larger dishes are necessary. In the case of pudding bowls, I use a 1.1 litre (2pt) rather than a 1kg (2lb); it makes all the difference.

304 Q. Do I ever have to cover the top of the basin when cooking steamed puddings?

A. Yes. If you were making a suet pudding the top would require covering and the whole basin sealed into cling-film with a slit made in the top.

305 Q. Can I heat jam for spreading, using the microwave oven?

A. Yes, in the jar with lid removed. Heat for 30 sec intervals on HIGH.

306　Q. Can I melt chocolate for coating in the microwave oven?

A. Break a 225g (8oz) bar of milk chocolate into small pieces into a dish and add approximately 1×15ml tbsp (1tbsp) milk. Heat on HIGH setting for appoximately 1 min. Stir thoroughly. If plain chocolate—melt alone—but stand 1 eggcupful of water on turntable.

307　Q. How do I make a rice pudding?

A. Grease a large dish; add 550ml (1pt) cold milk, 75g (3oz) rice, and sugar to taste. Stir well. Cook on HIGH for 5 min, then on SIMMER for 30 min. Stir three times during cooking. Sprinkle with nutmeg. Alternatively, use your favourite recipe, but do remember to use a larger dish than normal.

308　Q. Why does my rice pudding rise up and down during cooking?

A. Because it is cooked using a low setting. To simulate a thermostat the machine switches on and off for preset times, eg SIMMER microwave is on for 20 sec and off for 40 sec in every minute. The rice pudding rises when the machine is on for 20 sec, drops again when the machine 'rests' for 40 sec.

309　Q. Whenever I make custard it boils over.

A. It will unless a larger jug is used. All milk-based foods boil rapidly in the microwave oven and it is better to use a 1.1 litre (2pt) jug for 550ml (1pt) of custard.

310　Q. Is it possible to make smooth non-lumpy custard in the microwave?

A. Yes. The secret is in the mixing stage. Mix custard powder, sugar and top of milk extra thoroughly, before adding remaining milk. A 550ml (1pt) mixture takes approximately 5–6 min on HIGH setting.

311 *Q.* Do you have a recipe for egg custard?

A. Yes this one is a favourite.

Egg Custard

425ml (¾pt) milk
3 eggs, size 3
1×15ml tbsp (1tbsp) sugar or to taste

Pour the milk into a jug. Heat on HIGH setting for 3 min. Beat the eggs and sugar together, pour into a greased 1.1 litre (2pt) oval pie dish.

Whisk the warmed milk into the egg mixture thoroughly. Place the pie dish into another dish—not metal—containing boiling water. The level of the hot water must reach the custard level in the smaller dish. Cook on HIGH for 6 min; leave to stand before serving, sprinkled with nutmeg (*serves 4*).

Fish

There is simply no better way of cooking fish than in a microwave oven. Goodness, texture and flavour are all retained, and the cooking odours are contained in the oven.

312 *Q.* I have tried to cook fish but it does not cook in the centre. Why?

A. You are not covering the dish.

313 *Q.* How would I cook a large whole fish? It would fit on the turntable but not turn around?

A. If your machine has a stirrer fan, the turntable plate can be removed, upturned or stopped (depending on the machine). Cook the fish as recipe states, turning manually twice. If your machine does not have an oven-sited fan, the fish will have to be filleted.

314 *Q.* In my cookbook it states that trout may be cooked whole from frozen. How would I add stuffing or lemon juice?

A. Cook frozen trout on HIGH setting for 1-2 min and it will then be defrosted. Add stuffing or dress as required, and continue cooking to total time given in recipe.

315 *Q.* Can I pot shrimps using the microwave oven?

A. Butter a ramekin, add prepared shrimps, season to taste. Put knob of butter on top. Heat on HIGH for 30 sec or until butter melts, leave to set. Garnish with parsley before serving.

316 *Q.* Is it possible to cook whitebait in the microwave oven?

A. Yes, by using the browning dish. Heat dish with 1×15ml tbsp (1tbsp) oil on HIGH for 5-6 min; add fish and cook for 5-6 min per 450g (1lb), turning once.

317 *Q.* How would I cook fish fingers? I have not yet bought a browning dish.

A. Cook between two plates, one acting as a lid. Cook for 30 sec each if defrosted; 45 sec each if frozen, on HIGH setting. Several may be cooked at once.

318 *Q*. Can I cook breaded fish using the microwave oven?

A. Yes, but you will need a browning dish. Heat the browning dish with 2×15ml tbsp (2tbsp) oil added for 5–6 min on HIGH setting. Lower breaded fish into the browning dish. Allow 5–6 min on HIGH per 450g (1lb) of fish. Turn the fish over once to ensure even browning, then drain and serve.

319 *Q*. When using bought frozen cod steaks in a butter sauce, is it necessary to remove the plastic wrapping bags before cooking?

A. No. Slit the corner of the plastic packaging and place the whole packet onto a plate with a raised edge.

320 *Q*. Is it possible to cook kippers in a microwave oven?

A. Yes, and very successfully. Place kippers in a dish, dot each kipper with margarine or butter, cover and cook on HIGH setting for 4–5 min per 450g (1lb).

321 *Q*. Is it recommended to cook scampi in the microwave oven, or should I cook it conventionally?

A. Small amounts of scampi can be cooked in the same manner as breaded fish. Larger family-sized quantities should be cooked conventionally in deep fat.

Q. My familys's favourite seafood is crab. Can you recommend an original starter using crab?

A.
Crab Canapés

3 slices of toast, toasted conventionally and crusts removed
½×5ml tsp (½tsp) curry powder
seasoning to taste
1×5ml tsp (1tsp) lemon juice
½×5ml tsp (½tsp) tomato purée
150g (6oz) crabmeat, canned, fresh or frozen
75g (3oz) fresh mayonnaise
1 egg white, size 3, beaten until very stiff
prawns for decoration

Cover turntable with a piece of kitchen paper. Cut the slices of toast into 4. Mix the curry powder, seasoning, lemon juice and tomato purée, and add to the crab together with the mayonnaise. Fold in the beaten egg white. Spread the mixture over toast portions and cook immediately, directly on the turntable, in 2 batches of 6, on HIGH for 1–1½ min each batch. Serve immediately, decorated with prawns (*makes 12 canapés*).

Eggs and Cheese

Eggs and cheese form the basis of many recipes, and are valuable for nutrients as well as distinctive flavour. Use in recipes as you would conventionally.

323 *Q.* My friend tells me that scrambled eggs can be cooked in the microwave oven. How do eggs get the 'scrambled' look?

A. Using HIGH setting butter is melted first, before beaten eggs and milk are added. Stir once only during cooking, and the eggs magically scramble themselves when finally stirred after cooking is complete. 2 eggs take approximately 1½ min.

324 *Q.* Can I add salt to scrambled eggs before cooking?

A. Yes.

325 *Q.* Why do cookbooks suggest using a Pyrex jug for scrambled eggs?

A. Because its handle helps when stirring during cooking, and because Pyrex is clear, enabling the egg mixture to be watched as it cooks.

326 *Q.* Is it possible to cook an omelette using the microwave oven?

A. Yes, but you will need a browning dish.

Omelette
1×5ml tsp (1tsp) butter
2 eggs
seasoning
cheese for sprinkling (optional)

Heat the browning dish on HIGH setting for 5 min. Add butter and melt on HIGH setting for 15–20 sec. Lightly beat eggs and seasoning together, pour into the browning dish and heat on HIGH setting for 20–30 sec. With a fork, lightly draw the outer part of the egg into the centre. Heat again for 20–30 sec, repeating the process until the omelette is cooked. Sprinkle with cheese if desired.

327 *Q*. Is it possible to fry an egg in a microwave?

A. Yes, using the browning dish. Heat 1×15ml tbsp (1tbsp) oil on HIGH for 3–3½ min. Break egg into hot fat. Cook 15–20 sec on HIGH setting.

328 *Q*. My cookbook advises not to boil an egg. Why?

A. Any food with a skin or shell is best 'pricked' to allow hot air to escape during cooking, otherwise there is a build-up and the skin or shell explodes. One cannot easily pierce the shell of an egg. Boil it conventionally.

329 *Q*. Is it possible to boil an egg in the microwave oven?

A. Yes, but rather impractical. Wrap the egg in aluminium foil and immerse in a small basin of water. Heat water for approx 3½ min on HIGH setting.

330 *Q*. Why do my poached eggs explode?

A. Any food that has a skin will explode if heated too much. Though some books recommend it, I never 'pierce' eggs. Try using 1×15ml tbsp (1tbsp) water and a few drops of vinegar or ½×5ml tsp (½tsp) margarine or butter. Heat on HIGH for 30 sec, add egg, then microwave on HIGH for 30 sec.

CHEESE DISHES

331 *Q*. Can I melt cheese for topping toast using the microwave oven?

A. Yes. Slice amount of cheese required onto a plate. Microwave on HIGH setting until it melts.

332 *Q*. Is it possible to make French-loaf pizzas, topped with cheese, using the microwave oven for the whole process?

A. Follow recipe for Katie's Pizza (Q279), using French loaf instead of a scone base.

333 Q. My family's favourite dish is Moussaka. Can this be satisfactorily produced in the microwave oven?

A. **Moussaka**

2 large aubergines, thinly sliced
4×15ml tbsp (4tbsp) oil for frying
225g (8oz) onion, chopped
450g (1lb) cooked lamb, minced
1 small can of tomatoes, juice drained and discarded or 225g (8oz) fresh tomatoes, skinned and chopped
1×15ml tbsp (1tbsp) tomato purée
25g (1oz) butter or margarine
25g (1oz) flour
275ml (½pt) milk
75g (3oz) grated cheese
cheese for sprinkling

Cover aubergines with salt and leave to stand for a minimum of 1 hr, if possible. Heat the browning dish with the oil on HIGH setting for 6 min. Wash the salt from the aubergines and add them to the browning dish, cover the dish and fry gently until aubergines are quite soft—4–5 min approximately. Remove the aubergines and add the onions to the browning dish. Cook, covered, on HIGH setting for 4 min. Add to the meat, tomatoes and purée; mix well.

To make the sauce, melt the butter or margarine on HIGH setting for 1 min; add the flour, blend in a little milk, mix thoroughly. Heat on HIGH setting for 30 sec–1 min, stir. Add cheese and more milk and heat for 30 sec–1 min. Stir, add remaining milk and heat until mixture thickened, stirring regularly.

To Complete the Dish

Line the base of a 1.1 litre (2pt) casserole dish with most of the aubergines, then layer the meat followed by the cheese sauce until all is used up except a little cheese sauce. Topmost layer should be aubergines lightly covered with sauce.

Sprinkle with grated cheese, heat in the microwave oven on HIGH setting for 1–2 min. Flash dish under the conventional grill if desired (*serves 4–6*).

334 Q. Would scrambled egg cook well in the microwave oven, if I added 50g (2oz) cheese?

A. Perfectly well. Try also adding crumbled cooked streaky bacon.

335 Q. There is no recipe for cheese sauce in my book. Do you have one?

A.   **Cheese Sauce**
   25g (1oz) cornflour
   550ml (1pt) milk
   50g (2oz) grated cheese
   seasoning

Mix the cornflour to a smooth paste with a little of the milk. Gradually add the remaining milk and the grated cheese. Stir gently. Cook on HIGH setting for 3 min. Stir, then cook on HIGH setting for a further 2–3 min.

Pasta, Rice and Cereals

Whilst there is minimal time-saving in certain areas of cooking the above foods, results are superb and the methods clean and convenient—not to mention the lack of washing up after! Boiling water in a kettle first will speed the cooking process considerably.

Q. Could I cook lasagne in the microwave oven?

A. **Lasagne**

6 leaves lasagne
850ml (1½pt) boiling water
2×5ml tsp (2tsp) oil
salt and pepper to taste
25g (1oz) cornflour
550ml (1pt) milk
50g (2oz) grated cheese
600g (1½lb) lean minced beef
1 medium-sized onion, chopped
1 medium-sized can tomatoes
1 beef stock cube
2×10ml (2 dessertspoons) gravy granules, or
    25g (1oz) flour mixed with a little cold water
grated cheese for top
paprika

Lasagne Leaves
Place leaves into a deep dish (Wavecare
rectangular cover is ideal), add the boiling water,
oil and salt. Cook on HIGH setting, uncovered, for
8–10 min, gently immersing leaves by pressing
with a wooden spoon. Cook on HIGH setting for a
further 2–3 min. Press down with a wooden
spoon once more. Cook for a further 2–3 min on
HIGH. Put to one side.

Cheese Sauce
Mix the cornflour with a little of the milk and stir
to a smooth paste. Gradually add remainder of
milk and gently stir in the 50g (2oz) grated
cheese. Cook on HIGH setting for 3 min. Stir once
more, then cook for a further 2–3 min on HIGH.
Put to one side.

Meat Sauce
Cook the minced beef and onion together,
uncovered, on a HIGH setting for 6 min. Drain off
the surplus fat, then add the canned tomatoes and
their juice, crumbled stock cube, gravy granules
or flour and water, and seasoning. Cook, covered,
on HIGH setting for 15 min.

To Complete the Lasagne

Layer pasta and sauces in a 1.7 litre (3pt) large shallow dish in order of meat sauce, most of the cheese sauce, pasta—covering the topmost pasta layer with remaining cheese sauce and the grated cheese for decorating. Cook on HIGH setting for 4 min, then sprinkle with paprika for added colour (*serves 4–6*).

337 *Q.* I cooked long-grained rice and it boiled over leaving a sticky mess. Where did I go wrong?

A. Use a 2.3 litre (4pt) container to allow for bubbling up. If you have variable power, reduce to MEDIUM setting after water boils.

338 *Q.* I find that it takes too long to cook rice in the microwave oven, are there any short cuts?

A. Boil water first, using an electric kettle, before adding rice.

339 *Q.* Could I make Spaghetti Bolognese in the microwave oven?

A. **Spaghetti Bolognese**

Bolognese Sauce
450g (1lb) minced beef
1 onion, finely chopped
1 beef stock cube
1 small can tomatoes
seasoning to taste
100g (4oz) spaghetti
550ml (1pt) boiling salted water

Cook the beef and onion in a 1.1 litre (2pt) casserole dish, uncovered, on HIGH setting for 5 min. Drain off the fat, add remaining ingredients. Cook on HIGH setting, covered, for a further 13 min.

Spaghetti
Put the water into a large dish, gently lower in the spaghetti. Cook on a HIGH setting for 10 min, cover and leave to stand for 5 min. Drain, pour sauce over spaghetti, and serve (*serves 4*).

340 *Q.* How should I cook egg noodles?

A. For 225g (8oz) of noodles you will need a 4pt covered dish and 556ml (1pt) boiling salted water. Cook on HIGH setting for 5 min.

341 *Q.* Do you have a recipe for tagliatelle?

A.
Tagliatelle
225g (8oz) tagliatelle
1.75 litre (3pts) boiling salted water
2 egg yolks
4×15ml tbsp (4tbsp) single cream
50g (2oz) soft cream cheese
12g (½oz) Parmesan cheese
salt and pepper to taste
200g (8oz) cooked ham, cubed
2 spring onions, chopped
75g (3oz) chopped sweet peppers
knob of butter

Combine egg yolks, cream cheese, Parmesan and cream with seasoning until well blended. Meanwhile cook the tagliatelle in a large covered dish with the boiling water on HIGH setting for 4 min. Drain off the water and arrange the pasta in a shallow dish. Heat the cream mixture on HIGH setting for 2 min. Add the ham, spring onions and peppers to the cream sauce. Place the knob of butter chopped into small pieces on top of the noodles, pour the sauce over and serve immediately (*serves 4*).

342 *Q.* Can I make porridge in a cereal bowl in the microwave oven?

A. Yes, but make sure that the dish is deep enough as milk-based foods boil rapidly.

Soups

Home-made soups are a delight to serve and an effective way of using up left-overs. By combining the use of a freezer and microwave oven, soups can be prepared and stored for future use and will prove invaluable in meal planning as a starter instantly available, leaving the microwave oven free for preparation of the main course.

343 *Q.* I enjoy making soup for my family and would like some recipes. Can you help?

A. **Cream of Tomato Soup**
    1×800g (1lb 12oz) can of peeled tomatoes with
        their juice or equivalent weight of fresh
        tomatoes, skinned and chopped
    550ml (1pt) boiling water (if canned tomatoes
        are used 275ml (½pt) only)
    seasoning to taste
    1×15ml tbsp (1tbsp) demerara sugar
    generous dash of Worcester sauce
    50g (2oz) unsalted butter
    275ml (½pt) thick cream
    cream or parsley to garnish

Combine chopped tomatoes, water, seasoning, sugar and Worcester sauce in a 2.3 litre (4pt) covered casserole dish. Cook, covered, for 14 min on HIGH setting. Cool slightly, then press through a sieve. Return the purée to the casserole dish, stir well, adding the butter. Return dish to the microwave oven and cook on HIGH setting for 2 min. Gently whisk in the cream, heat on HIGH setting for 2 min. Serve hot or cold. Garnish with swirls of thinnish cream or parsley (*serves 6*).

Lentil Soup
    150g (6oz) lentils
    1.1 litre (2pt) stock (for best results cook a
        ham hock for 30 min on HIGH setting with
        1.1 litre (2pt) hot water)
    1 large onion
    2 sticks celery, chopped
    2 tomatoes, chopped
    1 bouquet garni
    50g (2oz) butter or margarine
    2–3×15ml tbsp (2–3tbsp) thick cream
    seasoning to taste
    parsley sprigs to garnish

Combine ingredients except butter, cream and seasoning in a large 2.3 litre (4pt) casserole dish with lid, and heat on HIGH setting for 25–30 min. Remove bouquet garni, and either liquidise mixture or pass it through a sieve (caution, with the liquidiser warm the jug first with hot water otherwise it might crack). Add butter or margarine and cream, season well. Return to the microwave oven on HIGH setting for 1–2 min. Decorate with parsley sprigs prior to serving (*serves 4–5*).

Minestrone Soup

1 can spring vegetable soup
550ml (1pt) hot water
1 small can of baked beans in tomato sauce
1×15ml tbsp (1tbsp) tomato purée
1 clove garlic, crushed or ½×5ml tsp (½tsp) minced garlic or garlic salt
25g (1oz) spaghetti, broken into small pieces
seasoning to taste
Parmesan cheese for garnish

Combine all ingredients. Cook in a 2.3 litre (4pt) covered casserole dish on HIGH setting for 20–22 min, or until pasta is softened. Serve in individual dishes, sprinkled with Parmesan cheese (serves 4).

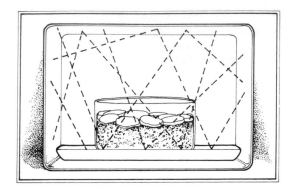

For the Technically Minded

Successful microwave cooking is based on a fundamental knowledge of how the machine operates. If you are about to buy a microwave oven, this section should prove invaluable.

344 *Q*. How far into the food do microwaves penetrate?

A. About 15 to 20mm (½–¾in) only.

345 *Q*. What is a magnetron?

A. It is one of the major components in any microwave oven. Its function is to pass microwaves into the metal cavity.

346 *Q*. What is a prism?

A. A prism is a static metal bar fitted into the roof of the microwave interior, to encourage microwaves to reflect off the microwave oven walls.

347 *Q*. What are cold spots?

A. Parts of the microwave oven which do not get as much concentration of microwaves as others.

348 *Q*. Do all ovens have cold spots?

A. Not any more. The efficiency of the stirrer fan and turntable combined has largely eliminated them

349 *Q*. Why is it unnecessary to preheat a microwave oven?

A. Because the cavity of a microwave oven never gets hot.

350 *Q*. Where is the seal on the door?

A. It is the rectangular metal framing the glass in the door. Metal is the only substance that microwaves cannot penetrate. Rubber, for example, would be useless, as microwaves would pass straight through.

351 *Q*. Is it possible for microwaves to leak out from around the door after lots of use?

A. Nothing is impossible, but the experts rate the chances of radiation harm from a microwave oven as the same as getting a suntan from the moon.

352   *Q.* What would happen if overspills got into the turntable mechanism?

      A. This is very unlikely as the glass tray holds 550ml (¾pt) of liquid even though only very small amounts of liquid are used in microwave cookery. The area is generally sealed.

353   *Q.* Is it normal for steam to be seen escaping from the door edge during the cook-cycle?

      A. Yes, and it is perfectly safe and acceptable for this to happen. Microwaves cannot escape with the steam as they only travel in straight lines.

354   *Q.* I can see the interior light through the sides of the door. Is it safe?

      A. Yes, microwaves cannot pass from the oven through a crack in the door only large enough to show light.

355   *Q.* My microwave oven makes quite a noise when the door is open, but my friend's doesn't. What is the difference?

      A. Some machines have a fan that works as soon as the door opens. Others only operate when the start button is touched. In practice there is no difference.

356   *Q.* I note from the specification of my appliance, that the machine is 650 watts. What fuse should I use?

      A. Whilst the output of your oven is only 650 watts the input could be as much as 1.4kW, therefore it is essential that you use a 13amp fuse.

357   *Q.* If I break the glass turntable can it be replaced and is it expensive?

      A. The plate is easily obtained from microwave stockists. Prices vary around £20.

358 Q. My microwave oven is a manual type machine. Using a time switch, could I programme it for the machine to switch on in my absence?

A. Yes. Set the machine up and press the starter. At pre-set time the microwave will start to cook, then switch itself off after cooking.

359 Q. My microwave oven has a clock. Does it matter if the machine is unplugged when not in use, and the clock is not set to proper time at each use?

A. No, since timing will still register for correct amount selected regardless of the time of day.

360 Q. If I set the timer for 10 min then open the door after 5 min, will I need to reset the timer?

A. No. The timer is arrested and will not start again until the 'start' operation is touched.

361 Q. My microwave is marvellous! If I decided to buy a second one, is it permissible to stack them one on top of the other?

A. Yes. Many cafés and pubs do this.

362 Q. My cookbook mentions molecular activity. What is it?

A. It simply means the microwaves' movement through food.

363 Q. Is it possible to use the microwave oven without the turntable?

A. Yes, but only if the machine has a stirrer fan in the roof to turn the microwaves in the absence of the turntable.

364 Q. Why is the inside of the microwave oven metal if I am not supposed to use metal dishes?

A. Microwaves bounce off metal, therefore to conduct movement of waves into food the inside has to be metal.

365 *Q*. Why do some microwave ovens have a metal turntable?

A. Generally speaking, a metal turntable is supplied with convection ovens where glass or ceramic would break under heat.

366 *Q*. My microwave oven is supposed to have a stirrer fan. Where is it, as I cannot see it?

A. Usually the stirrer fan is situated behind a plastic shield for purposes of simple cleaning.

367 *Q*. I have seen a temperature probe used in cooking jam and it seemed efficient. Can I buy one and fit it?

A. No. A temperature probe is an integral part of certain machines that are manufactured to cook by temperature and/or weight.

368 *Q*. What happens when the lightbulb burns out? Does the machine still work? Who replaces it and how?

A. The lightbulb's function is purely to illuminate the cavity during cooking. It is advisable to have an experienced microwave engineer fit the replacement bulb. Check with your warranty, because the turntable plate and bulb are rarely covered. *Some* additional warranty premiums cover everything, and these are generally available from microwave specialists rather than from department stores.

Also Available

BEGINNING MICROWAVE COOKERY

Margaret Weale

Microwave cookery is different. Understanding and accepting this simple statement will prevent tears of frustration for the new microwave cook. Though most buyers of microwave ovens are experienced cooks who want to learn the new techniques quickly and without failures, many of the cookbooks available make easy learning difficult by having long and complicated explanations of the theory of microwave energy. Few read them properly and anyway soon forget. The recipes assume this knowledge and important steps for the inexperienced are left out— with disappointing results.

This book is different. Margaret Weale has many years of experience of microwave cooking as a wife and mother and also as a home economist with a leading oven manufacturer. She has recognised the needs of the new microwave oven owner and arranged the chapters so that simple beginnings ensure successful result from the outset. Each recipe is complete and reminds the cook of the essential do's and don'ts. The step-by-step instructions leave nothing to chance and the charts on Defrosting, Reheating and Freezer to Table are invaluable.

The author has test-cooked every recipe and supervised the colour photographs taken by her husband Stan.

Colour photographs throughout

£3.95 net

ISBN 0 948432 05 5

ANGELL EDITIONS
Newton Abbot, Devon